Smart Marketing.
Take your business to the next level.

by Kerrie L. Cooper

www.kerrielcooper.com

Smart Marketing.
Take your business to the next level.
[By taking the first step: developing your marketing strategy.]
Expert guidance for entrepreneurs, creatives and small businesses.

By
Kerrie L. Cooper

big brand strategies for small businesses.

My clients typically arrive at my door at a critical stage in their growth: their sales have plateaued and they don't know why. They've built their business with pure sweat equity, relationships and sales. They are a $1 million dollar company and they wish to be a $5 million dollar company; an $80 million dollar company wanting to grow to a $120 million dollar company. If only they had the right marketing strategy to take them to the next level.

This is the where the work I do for them begins.

Written for the business owner, entrepreneur, sole proprietor, anyone in the creative world or the voracious reader who wants to know more about marketing. In this book you will learn a process which is the culmination of a lifetime career in marketing; guiding brands of all shapes and sizes toward achieving their goals.

This is where your work should begin.

To Paul Stanley, who gave me the opportunity and education of a lifetime.

To my wickedly talented husband and soul mate Michael DeMay, you are my best friend, editor and sounding board.

To my perfectly enchanting daughter Isabella, thank you for choosing me to be your mom. I will always love you more than ice cream.

What a marketing strategy can do for you.

A marketing strategy is a critical component to any successful business. Whether you are a company of one or one hundred, a proper marketing strategy can set you apart from the competition and help you bring your goals to fruition. It is a fundamental core element that serves to eliminate trial and error (otherwise known as throwing something against the wall to see if it will stick) or reactionary decisions (say, succumbing to the pressure of an aggressive ad sales person who has relentlessly stalked you); both practices tend to waste money and not produce results.

The process of creating a marketing strategy provides the opportunity to be the visionary you wanted to be when you embarked on launching your own business in the first place. It forces you to work <u>on</u> your business as opposed to being mired down in the muck of day-to-day tasks that in essence equates to you working <u>at</u> your <u>job</u> instead of working <u>on</u> your <u>business</u>.

Within this book I will provide the guidance you need to effectively brand and market your business. I have worked with numerous startups, entrepreneurs and small to mid-size businesses in this capacity for many years, and have developed an approach and methodology that simplifies the process. And while you may need to turn to outside resources to execute your plan, such as a graphic designer or web developer, I have every confidence that you can create a great plan if you simply follow the outline of steps provided.

So, why do you need to do this work, anyway? You may be saying to yourself, I've got a website, what else is there to do? Just because you have built it, doesn't mean they will come, much less buy from you. Compare this investment of time and money into your business to the time and money you'd invest in a building a new home. Let's say that you are building your dream home. You've defined your budget, made your wish list and are ready to go. Would you just write the builder a check and cross your fingers that it all comes out exactly how you want? My guess is no, you would not. Most people start with a plan. You'd hire an architect to map it all out. In my language, this is what a marketing strategy is – a plan.

That's what this process will do. Map it all out for you. So to continue with this construction analogy, a good strategic marketer is like a good architect. A builder is the person who will be executing the plan devised by the architect. Just like a graphic designer is the person who will take the strategy and create the visuals – we call it the look and feel – of the brand. Everyone needs to work from the strategic plan; otherwise, like any endeavor that requires creativity, the work can become too subjective.

Most small businesses and start-ups that I have advised over the years do not have lavish marketing budgets. This means that each marketing effort or tactic that you implement must be spot on. And this demands a well-thought out marketing strategy. So whether you are building a house or building a business, taking the time to invest in a great plan ensures not only a solid foundation, but also a successful end result.

When to create or update your marketing strategy.

New businesses and start-ups should create their marketing strategy prior to seeking funding or launching. Oftentimes a solid marketing strategy can replace the need for a costly business plan if it is coupled with a strong financial projection and analysis. Investors like to see that you have determined where you fit in the marketplace, what your unique positioning is, and how you intend on selling your product or service. Just remember, if you are a start-up, your marketing strategy will need to remain fluid, especially in the first year. Things can change quickly, and you don't want to invest your marketing budget in long-term commitments of any kind. Review your marketing efforts every quarter to ensure that you are on target and that your content is resonating with your desired audience(s).

If your business is already up and running, the marketing strategy should be reviewed and updated annually. You have the benefit of analyzing data and assessing what is delivering results and what isn't. If social media is a large part of your marketing mix, you should be staying on top of these initiatives quarterly, as changes to this particular marketing segment are frequent.

Ideally, you have a marketing professional on your team. If not, I would highly encourage you to use this series as a guideline, and retain the outside professionals you will need to help you implement the plan. Most importantly, follow the plan and do not deviate until you have a full year of metrics and data.

Before you begin, please know that there are some pitfalls that you should avoid. These are common problems that take place in the planning process primarily because you either A) aren't being honest with yourself or B) don't wish to take the time to do this work as thoroughly as it requires. Here are top three things that will get in the way of a good strategy (so don't do them):

> 1. **Don't do this**: You have lost touch with your customers and do not understand their wants and needs. The last time you communicated with them was the holiday season when you sent them a greeting card. You have made assumptions about them, perhaps even gotten into the habit of stereotyping them. **Do this:** Reach out to your audience to make sure you still know what their needs are and how they like to do business with you.
>
> 2. **Don't do this:** You develop your marketing strategy within the confines of your office without the benefit of

knowing what trends are taking place in your industry and what your competition is up to. **Do this:** When you approach the work of building your marketing strategy, a more comprehensive look into your industry is required. Look at great examples of marketing communications your competition is using by checking out their websites and their social media pages. Compile a year's worth of industry sales data and compare it to yours. Give your company a 360 analysis and uncover all of the internal and external issues – and be brutally honest. Look for articles from leaders who have been there before you and seek insights from them.

3. **Don't do this:** You set unrealistic goals or arbitrarily assign goals to departments or sales teams. **Do this:** Those who are going to be working on implementing the plan need to be involved in both the development of the plan as well as goal setting in order to be invested in the work. Ask yourselves and your team the tough questions on what is reasonable to achieve within the year. Then put forth a set of goals that everyone agrees upon and get the buy-in of your team.

Here is a true story that I can share with you that touches on each of these points:

A high-profile cancer center reached out to me to write a strategic brief for them that would help them reverse a three-year record of declining referrals. The facility attracts patients primarily through referrals from oncologists in four neighboring states. Over the course of the last several years, their referrals were slipping, and their Chief of Oncology wanted a plan to boost awareness and referrals.

I asked him to describe to me how they have historically communicated with these referral sources, which are, in essence, their primary customer. I learned that save for a brochure that they had created and sent via direct mail two years ago, there had been no communication at all.

I then asked him who was responsible for managing their database and making sure that the contact information at each of these facilities was still accurate. He could not recall if ever they had looked at their database.

We spoke about the cancer center itself – has there been anything new added to their treatments or protocols since the brochure was created? I asked. Yes, as a matter of fact, they had added a children's bone marrow transplant program.

Finally, we spoke about the Chief's insights on how he thought the clinic was perceived. I learned about a public relations snafu that had transpired three years ago, something that was proven untrue, but the news had been negative and may have left a lasting impression. However, from the Chief's perspective, this really wasn't a big deal.

My client wanted a plan. He was asking for a marketing strategy that would help them reverse the decline and grow awareness. Yet it was clear that they had lost touch with their customers and were perhaps making some assumptions about them. In addition, he was asking that the plan guarantee that they would increase their referrals by 30% in the first year, an unrealistic goal considering we did not know the extent of our customers knowledge of the center, their sentiments about it and or the type of information they need and how they wish to receive it; nor did we have any successful historic marketing efforts that we could meld into our strategy.

The very first step needed before a strategic plan could be created was to speak directly with these oncologists to hear from them first hand what they needed to know about the facility and if there were any issues, including perception issues, that needed to be addressed. I informed the Chief that I would go and speak with these doctors myself. [This manner of qualitative research, by the way, should never be conducted by an internal member of your company. The most candid information can only be obtained by one who is objective and disassociated from any outcome.] Once I had this information, I could then build the marketing strategy which will now include relevant recommendations to meet the needs of the primary customer.

Within my first several meetings with these oncologists, I began hearing some reoccurring themes. Issues quickly rise to the surface in this type of endeavor provided you are asking the right questions in the right manner.

After meeting with oncologists in all four states, my theories were crystal clear. There were many recommendations in the report which preceded the brand strategy and marketing plan; however at the core of the problem was that this facility had, in essence, rested on its laurels and had not made much of an effort at all to reach out and communicate with their referring physicians in the last few years.

In the meantime, their equally competent and high-profile competition were not only staying in touch with these vital professionals, they were courting them - inviting them to their facilities to introduce them to new technologies, treating them to dinner and in general, building strong relationships. The competition had also begun marketing directly to patients, (something the medical community at the time was reluctant to do), thereby consistently building their brand and awareness across both audiences.

The lesson for you here is this: if in the process of refreshing or creating your marketing strategy you find that there are too many assumptions being made about who your audience is, what they want, and how they wish to interact with you, you need to uncover those answers first through qualitative research.

The entire project of building your marketing strategy from start to finish, if there is a concentrated effort, can be accomplished in as little as four to six weeks. The variables on the project timeline depend upon on how many individuals internally you need to involve in the process and whether or not any qualitative research is required at the onset.

Above all, remember this: the success of any marketing initiative begins with a well-educated strategy. In the words of Sun Tzu, Chinese military general, strategist and philosopher:

"Strategy without tactics is the slowest route to victory.
Tactics without strategy is the noise before defeat."

Building your marketing and brand strategy requires candid objectivity, research, analysis and the development of realistic goals and tactics. It necessitates the participation of those who will be executing the plan and the momentum achieved through a diligent timeline.

The art of a brand.

The word "brand" has its origins in branding cattle; that is using a hot iron stamp to burn a unique symbol into the skin to differentiate one person's cattle from another. Whether you are a new startup or a company that has been around for decades, analyzing the effectiveness of your brand should be part of your marketing strategy annually. Those of you who are launching a new company have a fresh clean slate, so I'll approach this section from their perspective.

In the marketing sense, your brand means much more than simply how your logo is designed. A successfully built brand has to filter through your organization at every level and be consistently demonstrated to your customers. Let's break it down to its simplest explanation: remember those awkward teenage years in high school? When our lives were consumed with establishing ourselves or trying simply to fit in? We began honing our individual brand way back then, and became adept at unconsciously figuring others out at a glance as well. When I was growing up, we had "jocks" and "brainiacs" and "burn-outs." Some people were in all three groups while others defied categorization of any kind. Admirably, some possessed that certain je ne sais quoi, yes? There was a certainty about some of those more well-defined personalities of our youth, but also something else, something that you couldn't put your finger on.

This is a good foundation for understanding what branding is all about. A brand is what you think and feel about a product, company or service in that split second that they enter your mind. A successful brand is one in which what you think about them is who they really are. Unfailingly.

If you own a small company, or are a sole proprietor, then you are your brand. If you lead or work for a big company, the hope of every owner and board member is that the company brand is exemplified to your customers each and every day.

Consider some of the largest, most recognizable brands in the world. What do you think of when you see Nike? Southwest Airlines? Apple? Google? (Which, by the way, is a form of marketing nirvana - when a company name grows to become the verb or noun used in our everyday vernacular. Not since Kleenex has anyone done it as successfully as Google.) These mega-brands have equally mega-budgets to put forth the type of brand marketing that permeates our brain while we sleep (Just do it!).

The real trick to successful branding (for those of you without mega-budgets) is when a company delivers all that they tell us they are in an effective, sincere, consistent way. That's when we, the customer, become brand-loyal, refusing to so much as look the other way at the competition.

So as you work this process I encourage you to focus on how the company (or individual) brand must truly resonate with all involved. There has to be harmony between the tangible and the intangible, otherwise the customer will sense something false even if they can't put their finger on it. You must deliver on who you say you are consistently. To create your brand means to figure out what you stand for, what you wish to be known for, and how you intend on demonstrating this to your clients or customers every time they come into contact with you. Here are some additional questions to ponder as you contemplate your brand:

1. What is your unique point of view or distinction? If your company is already established, take the time to deeply analyze this question: Is your unique point of view or distinction still relevant to your customer?

2. How do you wish to be perceived?

3. How are you currently perceived? Make sure you have relevant, recent data to support this answer.

4. Objectively consider how you fit in the marketplace. Take the time to visit your competition's website and understand how they are marketing and positioning themselves. Don't build your brand in a vacuum. Don't do anything in a vacuum. It's dark and dusty in there.

Then define with detail who you are, what you do and (this is most important) <u>how</u> you do it. A customer will always know if you aren't delivering true to your brand, because it means you aren't owning up to everything you say you are.

I hope you are inspired to do the work you need to do to develop a brand that has that certain je ne sais quoi. You can take your company from under the radar and make it memorable - unforgettable even. I call it the art of a brand. It is equal parts creativity, educated strategy, culture and implementation.

As I always tell my clients, building a great brand takes time. But every step along the way, counts.

Goal setting.

Now that you understand the benefits of developing your marketing strategy, I know you must be anxious to roll up your sleeves and get to work. Here's the absolute first step you must take: identifying your goals. You should have two categories: 1) Business goals and 2) Marketing goals. If you intend to develop new products, service offerings or expand into new territories over the next few years, then your longer term goals should absolutely be identified too, as: 3) Additional growth opportunities. Even if tactics and initiatives to support these additional growth opportunities are not immediately incorporated into your plan, identifying them now can sometimes prevent costly mistakes, such as building a website that won't support e-commerce when you eventually intend to sell branded merchandise online.

For most small businesses and entrepreneurs, goals and objectives are dictated by your budget and resources. Just know right now that its very tempting to be overly ambitious when you take the time for such an analytical approach to the year ahead. I caution you to not over-extend yourself in this goal setting process. Stick to two or three goals in each category. This can be hard for the entrepreneur with big plans and even bigger passion; however, the key here is to set realistic, measurable goals. Nothing is more frustrating than an over-the-top set of goals. Despite common sentiments otherwise, it is not "motivational" to set the bar so high that no one can actually achieve it - it's demoralizing.

The next step is to secure the buy-in of your key team, board members and those who are responsible for executing the plan. The importance of getting everyone on the same page at this stage cannot be emphasized enough. Here's a great example of why: I recently worked with a small company of just four individuals, three principles and one support staff. This company was generating $8 million a year in revenue, and wanted take their business to the next level and become a $10 - $15 million dollar company; something their closest local competitor had already achieved. They needed a strategy to get them there so they retained me to guide them through the process of professionally branding the company and developing a marketing plan to support their goals.

This client had never before sought professional marketing expertise, so I was excited to work with them knowing full well the great strides that could be achieved in a small amount of time. After all, when you jump into a pool and know just enough to keep your head above water to get to the other side, imagine what a skilled swim coach can do for you – you can learn the proper stroke to out-distance your competition. I said to myself, "Let the games begin!" and set to work with this first step: goal setting.

To arrive at a succinct list of goals, my approach is to interview each of the principles separately, privately and one-on-one. To ensure an open, honest dialogue I also guarantee anonymity at the onset. Over time I have developed a query that gets beyond the surface just enough to begin to understand what motivates an individual. It's a blend of personal and professional questions to help me understand how each person fits into the puzzle, as well as what they bring to the organization. We get very detailed about goals, both personal and professional; isn't it nice, after all, when you can achieve both?

It didn't come as a surprise when I discovered that each of the principles had very different ideas of where and how the company should grow. Each had their own territory and client base and they were all working fairly autonomously within their own scope of expertise. In three very candid interviews, I discovered three different professional styles, three different service offerings and three very different ideas of how to take the company to the next level.

Once this was brought to their attention, we were able to work together and prioritize their short and long term goals. Can you imagine how much more quickly this team could've achieved their financial ambitions if they were all on the same page from the beginning?

The lesson for you here is to get everyone to weigh in on your goals. Do not limit your query to the top-level executives, either, as everyone who is involved in the process of creating, developing or executing the plan will add value to your vision.

How a competitive analysis will shed light on YOU.

Analyzing your competition objectively is a critical component to your marketing strategy. It provides insight into what everyone else is saying about themselves, how they represent themselves and what they call out as their best distinguishing feature. How everyone else defines themselves and their expertise provides the information necessary to rise above the milieu, and not simply sing the same tune in a different key. This step in your marketing strategy gives you insight into how to brand and position yourself within your industry. In fact, it plays a large role in the process. After all, if every company in your industry says the same thing and looks the same way (and you'd be surprised how often this is the case) your potential customers will more often than not simply make their decision on whom to work with on price alone. There is so much that can be gleaned in this step! Let's get started.

Back in the day, the only means to size up the competition was covertly or through a sample of customers who fit a certain demographic and were paid to participate in a focus group. With a focus group, you the business owner and your team of professionals would stand behind smoked two-sided glass and try to discern how these folks felt about your products or services, oftentimes by comparing them to your competition's.

I will state it for the record - I am not a fan of focus groups. It seems that every time I participated in these studies, I would walk away dismayed by the dynamics that played out amongst the group. Inevitably you had someone who was very vocal and some who seldom offered an opinion. Mid-way through as everyone gets a bit more comfortable with one another, the stronger personalities would try to assume control. There is lobbying and discrediting and oftentimes it seemed that their motivations for being there were disingenuous. A great mediator is critical and I have seen some of the best at work to help circumvent the behaviors I am referencing. Yet in matters of asking opinions, it simply seems human nature to try and convince someone that you hold the right one.

Today you can best examine your competition online with their website, their press, social media, blog and more. A website is more often than not the first impression of your company and brand. And you can learn almost everything you need to know to assess how well your competition presents itself from a marketing perspective from their website alone.

On average, you will want to include four competitors in your analysis. I typically recommend to my clients that they name their top three largest competitors, and let me choose the fourth to include in the analysis. I do this for a few different reasons depending on the client. For example, a small business may only pick local competitors; however, what if regional growth has been identified as a key goal? My fourth pick in that instance would be a company that isn't on their radar yet. Another possibility is that my client has a very, very poor website and has yet to discover (or admit) this truth about themselves. In this case, it is an excellent opportunity to select one of the best examples of a company in their field doing it right – no matter where they are located. So, first: pick your top four competitors. I encourage you to look outside of your immediate area and find an example that is impressive to you regardless of whether or not they are your direct competitor.

This competitive assessment is conducted purely from a marketing perspective, so you will be analyzing how the company portrays the following: **Brand identity**, **Positioning**, **Messaging** and **Point of difference**. Here's what I mean by each, as well as some tips on what to look for:

Brand identity: Remember when I spoke about the definition of a brand and how it needs to be presented with integrity consistently throughout your marketing? A company's website is no exception. Think of what your expectations are when you arrive at a Ritz Carlton Hotel. Their brand is so well established that you will be gravely disappointed if everyone you come into contact with does not meet or exceed your every wish with a polite "my pleasure, ma'am/sir."

A website needs to reflect a company's brand not simply by what they say about themselves, but also by the overall <u>experience</u> of visiting the site. Consider how the site looks and feels. Where does your gaze ultimately settle? Is the site cluttered? Easy to navigate? Has it been updated or is it outdated? How do they use images to establish their brand? Is there unity between what the brand stands for and how it is presented? For example, if it's a technology company that postures itself as a leader in website platform solutions, yet it features a slow-loading flash presentation on the landing page, there is an obvious disconnect between what the company stands for and how it is presenting itself. The brand identity viewed through the lens of a website is as much about how the interaction makes you <u>feel</u> as it is about how it looks and what it says.

There is nothing subjective about this. A great example of a brand perfectly personified on their website is Apple. The site is easy to navigate, intuitive to use with clean lines and great product images. Learning about new products is just a click away to a video featuring the individuals who <u>made</u> the product, lending an air of authenticity and insight into how it got made. The result? You feel their passion and that gets you excited to buy the product! This brand identity is consistent and continuous throughout all of their presence. From their stores, to their packaging, to their content and so on.

Positioning. Next, you will examine how your competition has positioned itself. Positioning is how a company attempts to distinguish itself. When you consider how your competition does this, you have an opportunity to further set yourself apart. The positioning of a company is communicated through their content as well as the imagery they choose to use. If they've done their job right, they have chosen one or two key distinguishing features (free shipping and returns 365 days a year – Zappos) and have clearly promoted them throughout both visually and with text.

That's if they did it right. Oftentimes, your competition has missed the mark when it comes to establishing and communicating their positioning. Some examples of poor positioning statements for small businesses are "we're the oldest" or "we are the best." It is a common misstep – in an attempt to define where you fit in the marketplace, you instead state characteristics - essentially telling people what you want them to think of you.

Another common error is when core principles and beliefs are used as distinguishing features; such as saying that you will "exceed customer expectations with integrity." This is not a proper positioning statement. Now granted, you want to have your customers say these things about you, certainly. However, you have to demonstrate these things, not simply say them. Southwest Airlines has a simple positioning statement "We love to fly!" They demonstrate that position in everything they do, from their easy online booking service to the witty way they communicate the safety features of the plane.

So as you examine how well the competition defines and supports their position, think about what you do differently even if you are not the first to do it. Does your psychology practice only retain clinicians with their doctorate degree? Then you should say that. Do you give 30% of your proceeds to charity? Build your message and your brand around this. More and more in today's world, people want to do business with people who they like – and – who are like them. Discover who you are and then make sure that everything you say and do points to the true you.

Messaging. Let's move on to messaging. This refers to the language that is used to convey a company's brand and positioning. Here again, you may discover some repetitiveness in your industry. The real estate industry, for example, is often guilty of this. It's wrought with "trustworthy" agents who "love" what they do and "sell the most" homes in the area! If you look at ten websites of local real estate agents, I would bet that eight of them will say this. If I'm a buyer moving to your town from out of state, how am I to discern who will best meet my needs if literally everyone says the same thing about themselves? Effective messaging supports the brand's uniqueness, and uses the entire website to convey this at every opportunity without being redundant.

It is also important to ensure that the content speaks to your target audience effectively. If your buyers are highly educated surgeons and medical doctors, than the language you use should be elevated to their level. Examine the words that are chosen as much as the style of the language. Is the tone of the content conversational or formal? Witty or sincere? Now, in addition to determining how successfully your competition uses their messaging, give some thought to what your brand requires from a tone and style perspective.

The competitive analysis allows you to see what is happening in your industry. It's all about setting your company apart from the rest of the pack. Without fail, this effort has always provided absolute clarity for me when I am retained to build a marketing strategy for my clients. If you are candid, objective and honest with yourself, it should do the same for you. Let me know how it goes, will you?

Who are you talking to?

Most businesses market to more than one audience, either as a result of selling different products or services, or as a result of servicing different types of industries. In this part of your marketing strategy, you will identify each of your audiences and put them in priority. How you prioritize them is dictated by your goals and budget. For example, you may have identified a new service offering that you wish to concentrate on. Thus, you may wish to put this audience first or second on your list. Or you have determined you only have the budget to focus your marketing efforts on your primary audience which has historically proven to be your "bread and butter" or foundation of your business. Smart! Start there.

In this analysis, you will consider everything you know about each audience and detail their characteristics, wants and needs. Why is this important? First, it ensures you are in touch with those you are marketing to. People change constantly, and they way individuals want to interact with you changes as well. Secondly, it allows you to address any assumptions you may have made about your audience, or shed a light on anything that you <u>don't</u> know about your audience. You may discover you need some new information about a particular audience because the information you have is outdated or not relevant any longer.

On the following page, I provide an example of an audience analysis that was completed for a real estate brokerage company. In this case, there are only two target audiences, real estate agents and the consumer themselves. It is not unusual, however, to have a third or tertiary audience as well. For example, an insurance company may sell primarily to the government sector, but also sells to hospitals. In their goal setting, they identified a plan to sell one of their products online. This is an entirely new audience for them, one that they will have to research first to determine who this target audience is and how they wish to engage with this company online. Back to the real estate brokerage example, here's the at-a-glance analysis:

Audience Analysis.

Audience | Agents	Audience | Sellers and buyers
PRIMARY	SECONDARY

75% female in this market 35 - 45 years old at least ten years experience men are mid-forties most have some college second or third career for most	primarily women searching (buyers) 35 years and up (sellers and buyers) average Nashville income is $68,000* *2009 US Census Bureau
Profile | Characteristics	**Profile | Characteristics**
advanced, independent, savvy its hard work and they know it passionate about what they do they resist change they have fear about economy brokerages work to convince their agents that they are nothing without their brand one of their biggest concerns is that by making a change, they will lose the business they are presently working on	technologically savvy 88% use internet to find a home* presently, it is difficult getting approved for loan statistics indicate that consumers will not remember the name of the brokerage house after two years (although they will remember agent) * Source: 2011 National Association of REALTORS® Member Profile
Wants | Needs	**Wants | Needs**
they need money they want to not have to work so hard to obtain a reasonable income they do not want change: consider changing brokerage houses "complicated" want more training, especially in social media marketing	they want to negotiate rates they want to make the best use of their time (which is why they search online) they want their realtor to understand their needs perfectly

Distinguish your company from the competition.

Now that you have examined how your competition defines themselves and their expertise, you have the information necessary to rise above the milieu and not simply sing the same tune in a different key.

If you have managed to remain objective throughout your work, you should have had at least one "ah-ha" moment. In my experience, there is usually more than one epiphany during this process. Things should have clarified considerably for you, and perhaps one or more critical points or truths have risen to the top. Here are a few defining moments I have uncovered and led my clients to in my work over the years:

A large healthcare service provider was enlightened when they discovered that their point of entry at hospitals had changed from a charge nurse to a nurse educator (or director of education). These are two vastly different audiences who speak different languages and have different objectives in their roles. Not only is <u>what</u> you say to them important but <u>how</u> you communicate with them is too, as they each have different channels of communication at their disposal.

A landscape designer in Austin, Texas was struggling with her brand. The competition in her area was growing and she no longer understood how to distinguish her work from everyone else. As I researched each of the competitors in her market, I discovered that most of the competition were businesses that were less than five years old. She truly could tout that she had been serving her area longer than anyone else (30 years) and this was a great distinction. Equally as significant was the awareness that her niche expertise was rare as well. She was one of only three other landscape designers who specialized in formal English gardens.

A real estate company discovered that their closest competitor had the same color scheme in their logo and on their website, making it difficult to discern between the two companies. Even their "For Sale" signs looked alike. This discovery prompted an overhaul of the design of their brand, creating distance from this competitor with an entirely new look and feel.

Sometimes what you shouldn't say about your company is even clearer than what you should say. In every strategy I create, I include a list of "do not use" words. They can be found in every industry and are words that are a part of the vernacular. They are overused and are to be avoided at all costs. You will know them when you see them, words like "trust" "integrity" and "experienced." Bleh! If you feel compelled to tell people you are these things, I am compelled to not believe you.

As noted earlier, many industries replicate themselves unknowingly by using the same content, look and feel to describe themselves. For example, if you look at any company in the healthcare industry, chances are the color blue will be prominent on their website. Ask yourself: do you want to blend in? Or stand out? Hopefully you answered "stand out." As my esteemed associate Joe Calloway states: You want to be the red apple in a sea of green. Check out: Becoming a Category of One.

Try and encapsulate your competitive advantage in a few words or a short sentence. The point of distinction I use in my marketing is "Big brand strategies for small brands." What sets you apart from all the rest? Be candid, be ruthlessly honest and most of all, make sure you can deliver on your word.

Brand filters.

If you have been taking notes so far, you fully understand the why behind this process, which is this: the success of any marketing initiative begins with a well-educated strategy.

You also know that this work requires candid objectivity, research, analysis and the development of realistic goals and tactics. And that this work requires the participation of those who will be executing the plan and the momentum achieved through a diligent timeline. The final product - your marketing and brand strategy - becomes the guide for all who work with you in the marketing and sales realm, providing the proper filter restraints and strategic foundation to all creative endeavors.

In this chapter, we will talk about the proper filter restraints. They are called Brand Filters and they were introduced to me years ago by an exceptional graphic designer by the name of Wendy Stamberger. To me, Brand Filters are the intersection of creativity and strategy. They are developed to authentically convey the brand in look and feel. It's a screening criteria and guides the development of all creative marketing elements and tools.

The concept of a filter is not unlike a lens. You view all of your marketing tools through this lens to ensure your creative is on point. Brand filters are merely descriptive words, adjectives, that breath life into a brand. I always shoot for between three and five brand descriptors with my clients, and I also choose the selected meaning or definition I am striving for. Here's an example of brand filters chosen for a technology company who develops applications for mobile devices:

1. **Precision.** exact, accurate, technical refinement
2. **Fresh.** new, different, original
3. **Reliable.** consistently good quality and performance, trustworthy
4. **Usability.** convenient, intuitive, user-friendly
5. Elegant. inventive, smart, pleasingly ingenious, simple

These filters are just one component of defining your brand, but they are an important part, as any design work - whether that is your logo design or the look and feel of your website - can be a subjective endeavor. Brand filters aide in taking the subjectivity out of the creative process.

In the beginning of your work in developing your marketing strategy, I spoke about interviewing all of the principals and leaders of an organization to ascertain what they felt were the goals and objectives of the brand for the year. Another question to ask everyone would be to describe the brand using between three and five adjectives. This will help you arrive at the proper filters.

Here's an exercise for you to further demonstrate brand filters. Pair up these adjectives with the appropriate brand. I gathered these words from their corporate websites, so this is merely my take on some suggested filters. Here they are:

1. elegance, prestige, luxury
2. handcrafted, artistic, sophisticated, human, enduring
3. imaginative, intuitive, stylish, cool, casual
4. design, functionality, low-price

Here are the companies: Ikea, Starbucks, Rolex, Apple. Think about what each brand represents to you and the words you would use to describe each brand. You will find the answers at the end of this book.

The best investment of your marketing dollars.

There are many tools that can be used to communicate to your target audiences. To determine where the best investment of your marketing dollars should be placed, the first step is to assess which tools you will be using to communicate to your customers. Start with the most important tool and then prioritize the rest of this list:

- ✓ Website
- ✓ Digital media
- ✓ Email marketing
- ✓ Collateral pieces
- ✓ Videos
- ✓ Social media
- ✓ Trade show presentations
- ✓ Traditional media (radio, television, print, outdoor)
- ✓ Public relations

If you are a new business or a start-up seeking investors, you will still need to prioritize this list; however, you will also need to take the additional step of obtaining estimates to build these tools for your marketing arsenal. After your budget to build the tools is created, you can then follow the rest of the steps outlined below to identify and prioritize the tactics in your marketing strategy.

There are many potential components to a marketing strategy, and every company will create their own strategy to achieve their defined goals. Determining where you marketing dollars should go is a bit like putting the pieces of a puzzle together.

The list below identifies tactics that are typically the most cost effective (although may be labor intensive) as well as initiatives that tend to require a larger budget to achieve results:

- ✓ Branded email campaigns | cost effective, labor intensive, requires skill
- ✓ Social media | cost effective, labor intensive, requires skill
- ✓ Digital media | cost effective, requires expertise
- ✓ Public relations | requires expertise, requires investment
- ✓ Promotions or Co-promotions | requires expertise, can require bigger investment
- ✓ Traditional advertising | requires larger budget and longer term commitments
- ✓ Trade shows and conventions | requires initial large investment into booth/tools

✓ Direct mail | can be cost effective but less targeted and trackable
✓ Sponsorship | good for brand building, runs the gamut of investment

If you have historical data available to you on marketing initiatives that have worked for you in the past, this part of your process will be a little easier. If not, then be prepared for a year of testing. You can consider it your trial and error period, although with outside expertise you may be able to mitigate some of your margin for error.

To help guide you, I will take each marketing initiative and outline some of the pros and cons you can expect from them.

The world of digital media (email, social media, Google Ad Words and other digital media) can be scaled most effectively and when combined with other tactics can create an effective marketing strategy without a sizable investment. For example, you can send unlimited, professionally branded emails to a database of 2500 contacts for $45 a month through local email marketing company **My Emma**. Similarly, you can create an effective Google Ad Words campaign for as little as $350/month.

Social media deserves its own call out, as many may erroneously think that this one component can make or break the success of their endeavor. These platforms are crowded and ever evolving, and require attention and possibly immediate responses virtually 24/7. The great thing about social media is that, although the demographics of any one platform are very specific (but may shift), there is great data available for these sites. You can find out who is using the site, the amount of time they spend on it daily and when peak periods are. The key to effective social media campaigns lies in offering valuable content to your audience that doesn't resemble advertising and integrating your efforts with other marketing initiatives.

Public relations is another often misunderstood marketing tool. Many think of PR as simply a way to get into the local media via miscellaneous Press Releases touting a new hire, shattering a sales record, or announcing an acquisition. These misguided endeavors require one missing component - a caring public. The Press Release serves its purpose, for sure, but as a stand alone, they will not garner you the media attention you are seeking (unless it is an incredibly slow day for news).

Public relations, by definition, is designed to promote the good works of a company. (When exactly it transitioned to equating to bragging rights, I couldn't tell you). Good works are when a company is generously contributing to their community or giving back in some way. Some brands have intertwined their good works seamlessly and flawlessly into their brands, like **Tom's Shoes** who's brand tagline is <u>One for One</u> - for every product purchased, they help someone in need. Also referred to as "Cause Marketing" this type of initiative, brand or company has become increasingly popular, particularly with Millennials (those born between 1982 and 2004), who value positive brand association and are more prone to becoming brand evangelists than Generation Y (born between 1980 and 1994) before them, who are defined as demonstrating no brand loyalty. [reference mccrindle research, **Generations Defined Sociologically**. Note: This chart is a bit dated, so you will have to do some math to update the age brackets defined, but it is a great reference tool to better understand these audience segments].

Promotions and co-promotions can be effective with lifestyle brands (for example: gatorade and sports) or brands that co-exist naturally well together (like popcorn and movies). Bounce-back campaigns driving consumers to a store for purchase or discount coupon offers are great tactics with promotions. Typically limited in the length of time they are offered, promotions are great for introducing new products or services but need to be supported with other communication to successfully get the word out.

When it comes to traditional advertising, (outdoor advertising, television, print or radio) these methods can be effective brand builders but typically require larger budgets to be successful. You may also need to invest long-term with a particular media outlet to see results or achieve great rates (unless your advertisement if very targeted and short-term, such as a Memorial Day Sale that carries a specific call to action and a limited window of opportunity). Knowing your audience here is crucial as well. Many 20, 30 and 40 year olds no longer watch, listen or pay attention to traditional media. So if this is your buying public, this will not be a wise investment for you.

Trade shows and conventions are still really popular with B2B marketers, although there has been a discernible shift away from multi-million dollar booths and bringing the entire sales force out to Las Vegas. Previously, trade shows meant new contracts while in today's market it is generally viewed as a relationship building effort. Consumer trade shows may very well be hugely popular annual events, but here again, sales do not take place there. Rather they are viewed as information gathering events with many new products introduced. Investments here can be a costly investment up front with the building of a booth. Typically your investment will last two - four years before needing to be updated.

Direct mail is another tactic that once was an extremely popular and cost effective mode of marketing. Today's consumers typically toss anything remotely resembling "junk mail" and are less impressed with even the greatest "value" offering. Still, college recruiting and fundraising rely heavily on direct mail; as do local neighborhood restaurants and retailers.

Finally, sponsorship can be an effective tool in your arsenal provided it is integrated into campaigns that meet your goals versus merely paying for the privilege of associating with an event, artist or entertainer. Good sponsorship campaigns are much more than signage privileges and "brought to you by" announcements. And whether you are investing in a local golf sponsorship or a title sponsorship of the World Cup, the best results are achieved by leveraging the awareness of the opportunity, and ensuring you have a means to bring it down to the local level with initiatives and tactics designed to increase sales or traffic.

Determining the best investment of your marketing dollars will be an equation that is unique to you. A marketer's tools are the same whether we are introducing a new brand of dishwasher soap or we are launching a new public health care solution. The variables are in the audience you are trying to reach and the budget you have to achieve your goals. If you have a limited budget at the onset, pick two or three avenues to invest in; track and measure as you go along, but do not deviate from the plan for one year. Then assess your next step. If you have a larger budget, you will be well-served to deploy several initiatives and integrate your efforts thoroughly and consistently. Let's talk about integration, shall we?

Integrate your tactics.

Here's my favorite analogy about integrating your marketing tactics: picture a pristinely calm pond in the middle of a clearing. People are gathered there, but most of them are looking away from the pond. Now enter the misguided business owner who wishes to dip their big toe into the world of marketing. So he purchases an advertisement that appears in the paper three times. Each time the ad appears, envision a rock being thrown into the pond. Did you see the rock being thrown? See the ripple? Or just hear about it from someone? Chances are no one saw the rock in the first place.

To integrate your marketing efforts means not to rely on any one effort at a time, but rather tie them all together so that one plays off of and supports the other. This way, instead of one rock being thrown into the pond, you are actually making it rain. THAT's integrated marketing. No tactic should stand alone. It is a waste of your marketing investment.

Think about how you approach a purchase. When was the last time you went out to buy a new car? Did you just stroll into your local friendly dealership with your hands in your pockets and a smile on your face, prompted by the billboard you passed on the highway? Nah. Chances are you researched the type of car you wanted to buy. You may have been led by brand loyalty, or you may have been led by a Consumer Reports study of the safest SUV's. You actually shopped for your car in the comfort of your home (or office). Then you narrowed your choice down to two or three and then you went to the dealership for a test drive - or had the dealership bring the cars to you to test drive. The point is, you actively sought information about the purchase and took yourself through the bulk of the decision making process before you picked up the phone.

That's not just you. That's everyone. Today's consumer wants information about you. Free information. They want to learn about you and your product or service at their own pace, and the feedback or opinions of others plays a part in their decision. Marketing today is more about communication than it ever has been. So make sure it's available everywhere, not merely on your website. And when you do launch your marketing campaign, make the information you communicate helpful and valuable to your buying customer.

Implement your plan.

Now that you have decided the proprietary marketing mix for your strategy, it is time to implement your plan. The best advice I can give you in this part of the process is to map it out first. This helps ensure that you are being realistic in the amount of time it will take you to launch your plan, but more importantly, you can see the integration at play. Timing matters here, as does being responsive with customer service or inquiries, so make sure that you are properly staffed before you approach any endeavor. Below is sample of a year's implementation. This plan would require a marketing staff of at least four to implement it.

Sample Marketing Plan.

September	October	November	December

Q4 promotion Budgets Develop Content strategy Develop Website strategy Develop Mobile site strategy Develop PR strategy Develop Social media strategy Develop Digital Media strategy	Launch Q4 promotion Email campaign launch Buy in on: Content strategy Website strategy Mobile site strategy PR strategy Social media strategy Refresh website	SME campaign development PR templates built Social media pages built/ refreshed Mobile site development Market analysis examination	SME campaign development Q4 promotion results analysis Secure market analysis partner Photographer review
January	**February**	**March**	**April**
Content development PR/cause marketing Social media digital media SME blogs Promotion	Content development PR/cause marketing Social media digital media SME blogs Promotion	Content development PR/cause marketing Social media digital media SME blogs Promotion	Content development PR/cause marketing Social media digital media SME blogs Promotion
May	**June**	**July**	**August**
Content PR Social media digital media SME blogs Promotion	Content PR Social media digital media SME blogs Promotion	Content PR Social media digital media SME blogs Promotion	Content PR Social media digital media SME blogs Promotion

You will note the first month includes all of the strategic work for each initiative. And you thought all of your strategic work was over! Not so, my friend. You will need to create a strategic brief for each component of your plan. For example, if Social Media is in the marketing mix, you will need to define which platforms you are engaging with and ensure you have the proper content prepared for the launch. In fact, content is the current superhero in the marketing arena these days. Good content helps engage customers and starts relationships. So if you do not have a great marketing writer on staff, make sure you invest in one who can not only tell your story authentically, but can ensure that each medium has appropriate messaging as well.

I hope you have enjoyed this book as well as the process of developing your own marketing strategy. While this is no simple undertaking, a great marketing strategy and a well defined brand can truly be the difference between success and failure.

I wish you well as you embark on this work. Let me know how it goes for you, will you? As always, feel free to drop me a line with any questions you may have: k@kerrielcooper.com.

1. elegance, prestige, luxury (Rolex)
2. handcrafted, artistic, sophisticated, human, enduring (Starbucks)
3. imaginative, intuitive, stylish, cool, casual (Apple)
4. design, functionality, low-price (Ikea)

Biography.

I am a brand strategist, marketing guru and a writer. I blog on marketing and I blog on life. I was trained by the big brands and focus my practice and workshops to serve entrepreneurs with vision, other creatives in the marketing space and small business owners. I have worked in many different industries - from cancer centers to car manufacturers to ivy league schools; and with many different famous folk - from pop stars to legendary crooners, hat acts to cartoon characters and those little elves who make cookies. I know about launching and building brands and how to strategically integrate your marketing efforts for greater impact. I educate clients on how to grow sales, achieve market share and build brands that last.

I rose to the top of two marketing firms, first as Vice President in Detroit serving the top three automotive makers; then as General Manager in Chicago, working with widely-recognized brands such as AT&T, Nickelodeon Network, Procter & Gamble, Frito Lay, General Motors, ABC Television, Kraft Food Company, and House of Seagram's, along with a host of mega-entertainer brands running the gamut of music genres from Frank Sinatra to Tim McGraw; Tony Bennett to The Beach Boys; Herbie Hancock to Barry Manilow.

Working with and leading teams that created and launched new products or services under these behemoth corporations and entertainment conglomerates taught me how to become a household name. I have applied my skills to countless small to mid-size companies whose goals included both B2B and B2C marketing.

What I've learned through the years is this: Building a brand takes time. But each step along the way, counts.

www.ingramcontent.com/pod-product-compliance
Lightning Source LLC
Chambersburg PA
CBHW081306170526
45165CB00011B/3433